FROM THE *garden,* TO THE *Sea*

A Journey of Self Discovery

By
LILIANA LOPEZ

Photography by
MIEKO HORIKOSHI

This is a work of fiction. Names, characters, places, and incidents either are the product of the author's imagination or are used fictitiously. Any resemblance to actual persons, living or dead, events, or locales is entirely coincidental.

Copyright © 2020 by Liliana Lopez

All rights reserved. No part of this book may be reproduced or used in any manner without written permission of the copyright owner except for the use of quotations in a book review. For more information, address: info@thelilianalopez.com.

First paperback edition June 2020

Book design by Mieko Horikoshi
Photos by Mieko Horikosi

ISBN 978-1-7335263-2-6 (paperback)
Library of Congress Control Number: 2020910476

www.thelilianalopez.com

Acknowledgments

To my mother, Maria and sister Linda,
thank you for sharing your life with me.
I love you always.

— Liliana Lopez

To my mother Reiko,
and my daugthers Hana and Aya.

— Mieko Horikoshi

Table Of Contents

1. Prologue vii
2. By The Garden 1
3. The Kitchen 5
4. The Room 9
5. The Bath 13
6. A Nightmare 17
7. Goodbye 21
8. The Gas Station 25
9. The Road 29
10. The Diner 33
11. The Sky 37
12. The Road 41
13. The Hotel 45
14. A Dream 49
15. The Sea 53
16. Notes 57

Prologue

Life: The quality that distinguishes living organisms from dead organisms and lifeless matter, manifested in functions such as metabolism, growth, reproduction, and response to stimuli- the interval between birth and death.

If each of us defined life, what would our definitions be? Would they be similar to the dictionary's definition? Or would they take a life of their own?

My definition of life changes every time I get up in the morning. I learn something new every day, and for that, I am truly grateful. Everyone has a garden that needs pruning every minute of their lives. Whether we are conscious of it or not, we are planting new seeds all the time. As we sow, so we reap, sometimes we may not like what we reap. If we had realized at the time what we were sowing and changed, our gardens would have turned out differently.

We can go back to find where we made the wrong turn and ask ourselves, where did this weed come from? Why did I choose to plant it? Yet asking those questions will not bring us healing; instead, we must forgive ourselves and take the first step to refine our lives. To try and get back on that road where we can find our sea, our safe haven where innocence, peace, and love still exist. We take it with us everywhere we go; listen to that little voice within us called intuition.

We make our journey from our garden to our sea. Wherever that road leads, we must stay true to ourselves. To find our true path and live in the moment with joy every moment of our lives. I hope you enjoy this journey of poetry, where I have experienced part of my true path. I hope that in some way it helps you find your garden and sea.

Liliana Lopez

By The Garden

Sitting by the garden
plucking out the weeds,
trying to start all over
by planting new seeds.

Removing all the soil
that is spoiled and rotten,
trying to pull out old memories
That have been forgotten.

Pulling out the roots
that are buried deep inside,
looking all over for that
place they use to hide.

Here they come! One by one,
plucking out more than a dozen.
Trying to defrost the ones
that have been frozen.

Looking very careful,
which is old, which is new.
Trying to figure out
what is false, what is true.

As I look through the soil
and give it a squeeze,
I feel on my face
the soft, gentle breeze.

I hear the whisperings
and the cries of the woods.
I look at the weeds where
they once stubbornly stood.

I can feel my tears falling
down on my face.
What should I do with
this vast empty space?

What can I plant
in this forgotten garden?
What can I do, so
this soil won't harden?

How can I plant
these beautiful flowers?
Keep them growing and shelter
them from the harmful showers?

How can I stop
the weeds from coming back?
This feeling of loneliness,
this sense of lack.

Should I run, should I hide?
Should I ask for help? Should I try?
Can I do it alone or have someone by my side?
Do I wait and let the years pass me by?

But I won't,
I cannot wait any longer.
Staying in this limbo,
this place that is somber.

I must go, and I shall find.
That special place, that special me.
From the garden to the sea.
Where I can find where I can be.

The Kitchen

Upon entering the house,
I go straight to wash my hands.
Looking at some pictures
of the sea and white skin sands.

I feel the warmth of the sun
caressing my soul, caressing my body.
I hear the call of the waves,
telling me that I am somebody.

I realize there is something
wonderful, something new.
Growing deep inside of me,
something that I always knew.

But there is a feeling, a shadow.
Stopping it from surfacing, a block.
It feels really heavy
inside my soul, like a rock.

I try to face it.
I try to confront it,
but the thought of me alone!
I cannot condone it.

My hands! The heat of the water
has burned them. I feel pain.
I turn on the cold water
and watch through the window the rain.

Flashes! Happy faces of
little children together
singing a song of the rain
hoping it would stop forever.

Lighting! The fear of the children
on their faces, they are mad.
Wanting, hoping for the rain to stop,
but it would not, they are sad.

My hands! The coldness of the water
has frozen them. I feel numbness.
I sit on the chair,
inside this spell, this dumbness.

The earth is moving,
this uncontrollable shaking.
Me, in the midst of it!
How can I stop from not awakening?

I realize the earth is not moving at all.
It is me, a volcano inside of me,
ready to erupt and destroy
anything in its path. Me!

Get a hold of yourself.
I tiny voice cried.
I looked around to see
where it came from, but it had died.

My hands! Hot and cold.
My poor little hands.
Then I remembered the picture
of the sea and white skin sands.

I must go, and I shall find.
That special place, that special me.
From the garden to the sea.
Where I can find, where I can be.

The Room

As I climb the stairs
towards my room,
I open the door and
find a cloud of doom.

I look around and see
all the familiar things.
A medium bed, a chest made of wood,
and a tiny bell that rings.

A doll that has seen better days
dressed in white and blue,
a teddy bear that read
I will always be true.

My favorite pillow.
My favorite dress,
all of these things that
never made me feel any less.

I can feel the distance
and the pain in my heart,
of these material things
I know I must part.

A wave of loneliness
fills up my mind.
What am I doing?
I wish I could rewind.

Go back to my happy times
to those good old ways.
When I knew who I was,
in those good old days.

When a strangers smile
made my days bright,
when somebody else's
candle was my light.

When the actions
and words of a stranger
suited me perfect, like
clothing does on a hanger.

When the weather and moon
determined my mood,
when I knew who I was
and I knew where I stood.

When I valued myself
for all the things that I had.
For the image, I portrayed, for that
I never knew it was sad.

All I know it felt good then
and I wish it still did now,
perhaps I could close my eyes
and make it go away somehow.

But is too late for that
for I have seen the light.
The light that is within me,
it can make my days bright.

I must go, and I will find.
That special place, that special me.
From the garden to the sea.
Where I can find, where I can be.

The Bath

The sun is setting,
I must finish packing.
Walking through the dusk
wondering what I am lacking.

I turn the lights on
the whole room lights up.
I can feel the emptiness
from my toes on up.

I walk by the mirror
to make an observation.
Is this really me?
Or is it just my imagination?

I look at my face,
I look at my lips.
I take a good look at my body
and a good look at my hips.

I walk to the bathroom
wanting to be clean.
I turn on the water,
I don't want to be mean.

I feel the warm water
and light up some candles,
I take off my clothes
and take off my sandals.

I dim the lights
and step into the bathtub,
my muscles contract.
I need a back rub.

I lay down to relax,
to let myself go.
I close my eyes,
I feel it so.

I stretch out my left arm.
I stretch out my right arm.
I stretch out my legs,
trying not to harm.

I take the soap and a sponge
and begin to scrub my body,
cleansing the idea
that I am a nobody.

I take a look at my skin,
my poor skin, the color of red.
Its time for me to stop.
Its time for me to go to bed.

I finish washing up
I put on my towel.
I pull it real tight
and fasten the dowel.

I blow out the candles
and turn off the light.
I put on my pajamas and
lay on the bed. Good night.

I must go, and I must find
that special place, that special me.
From the garden to the sea.
Where I can find, where I can be.

A Nightmare

Somewhere in the distance
I could hear a sound,
then the bed was shaking
and I fell to the ground.

My head was spinning badly
and I felt in a daze.
I opened my eyes and
found myself inside a maze.

The maze was kind of dark
and it felt very cold,
the walls that held it
together looked very old.

I thought I saw a door
and ran very fast,
but it was just a sign
that read "The Past."

I couldn't understand
how I got to this place.
I tried to find an exit, but I
kept returning to the same space.

I tried to adjust my eyes
when I heard a click,
I look around and found two
doors. Which one should I pick?

The signs above the two doors
read "The Future," "The Past."
I didn't know which one to open.
Should I leave the past for last?

I opened the future door,
but there was nothing there.
I tried to go inside,
but I could not get anywhere.

I turned to the past door,
I was scared to go inside.
I looked all over for a
place where I could hide.

But the maze was getting smaller,
I didn't have a choice.
I opened the past door,
And could hear a little voice.

It sounded like a little girl
trying to find her way.
I could not see her face,
but I knew where she lay.

I wanted to come closer
to hold her in my arms,
I wanted to tell her
I didn't mean any harm.

I heard her speak.
You will be fine. Go!
I deeply understood that
little girl was me. I went slow.

I must go, and I will find.
That special place, that special me.
From the garden to the sea.
Where I can find, where I can be.

Goodbye

I could feel the sun
shining down on my face.
I opened my eyes and found
myself back at my place.

I laid there for a moment
and thought about last night.
The need for me to go
felt good. It felt right.

I didn't know where I was going,
I just knew it was meant to be.
I needed to find that special place
where I could finally be me.

I thought about not going
but the feeling was too strong,
I know I had a choice
between "right and wrong."

I got up very quickly.
I wanted to leave now
before my courage left me
and deserted me somehow.

It took about an hour
to get things done.
I wanted everything to be
perfect before I was gone.

I walked through the house
and took a look around.
I wanted to remember it all,
from the ceiling to the ground.

I went to the backyard
where I had my vision,
there laid my garden
full of hopes and ambitions.

I wanted to tend to it,
I wanted to stay.
I had to remind
myself to walk away.

When I came back,
my garden will still be there.
The thought offered me comfort
and removed all despair.

Still a sense of loneliness
filled up the place,
yet I knew now the
reason for the empty space.

Tears ran down my face,
Am I doing the right thing?
I had to leave now
before I tried to do something.

I locked my home
and wanted to shout.
Goodbye, goodbye.
The words would not come out.

I must go, and I will find.
That special place, that special me.
From the garden to the sea.
Where I can find, where I can be.

The Gas Station

I got inside my car
and started to drive away.
The rear-view mirror whispering to
me to look, telling me to stay.

The whispers went away
when they knew I wouldn't look.
Only if they knew all
the courage that it took.

Once out of my neighborhood,
I didn't know where to go.
Left? Straight? Right?
Left! A tiny voice said so.

I listened with distrust
but turned left anyway.
I knew I had to listen
to what the voice had to say.

I asked the voice a question.
Where do I go now?
The voice did not answer,
I needed to figure it out somehow.

I had to make a stop
to put gas in the car,
if I didn't do it now
I couldn't get too far.

Five miles down the road,
I saw a gas station.
It was very crowded
Everyone was going on vacation.

I had to wait in line
so I listened to a song,
it was about a couple
whose love was not too strong.

It was finally my turn,
I started to pump gas.
Who were all these people
waiting to pass?

Some were in a hurry;
others were frustrated.
Some looked very bored,
which was understated.

They were all going somewhere,
to a new location.
I wondered if they knew
where was their destination.

I wondered if they had
a tiny little voice
they could listen to,
when they had to make a choice.

        I finished pumping gas
        and got inside my car,
        I wanted to leave now.
        I needed to be afar.

    I must go, and I will find.
That special place, that special me.
  From the garden to the sea.
Where I can find, where I can be.

The Road

I drove down the highway
for about forty miles.
I saw many cars
many people with smiles.

Following the road
thinking of the choices I must make,
all the turns and exits
wondering which one was fake.

Stop thinking like that!
Always thinking of the bad.
What is true? What is false?
Always thinking of the sad.

For once in your life,
think of the good things.
Your home, your family,
and the tiny bell that rings.

It was a gift of love,
that tiny bell that rings.
When your mother hears it,
it makes her heart sing.

You keep looking for the bad,
leaving out the good.
Wondering what happened,
wondering where you once stood.

But the past is gone now
and you must drive on that road,
and try to stay on track
while you're trying to unload.

It may seem hard at first,
but you will get used to it in a while.
Just think of the good things
and that warm, bright smile.

The smile in your heart
that can make your days right,
the beautiful candle
that will always shine bright.

The beautiful garden
you are trying to revive,
so you can feel much better
and once again feel alive.

Let go of the old things
and get rid of the weeds.
Drive down this road
and collect new seeds.

I parked beside the road
to let the tears fall.
The volcano erupted
and broke down the walls.

I stood by the road,
don't know for how long.
Yet when I left
I felt more strong.

I must go, and I will find.
That special place, that special me.
From the garden to the sea.
Where I can find, where I can be.

The Diner

I was very hungry
and had to stop.
I could hear my stomach
shouting, I thought it would pop.

I saw in the distance
and older man dining.
I should eat there before
the sun stopped shining.

I parked the car
and went inside,
I tried to look for a
booth where I could hide.

The booths were all taken,
and I had but once choice.
Pick the main table in the middle.
"Stop complaining," said the little voice.

I was being childish,
I could not help it.
The thought of people watching me,
I could not take it.

I sat down anyway
and ordered some food.
How long will it take?
It all smelled really good.

I heard someone laughing.
Were they laughing at me?
I wanted to look, but
I was too scared to see.

The food was on the table,
and I wanted to eat.
I was very self-conscious
my heart skipped a beat.

Pick up the fork;
let yourself go.
I knew I could do it;
it had to be so.

With a deep sigh of relief
I started to eat,
the struggle within me
knew no defeat.

After a moment
I looked around,
nobody was watching me
there was not even a sound.

Happiness filled me.
I wanted to shout
I did it. I did it!
Everybody, look out!

The seeds for my garden
were filling my being.
My vision was clearer,
I was finally seeing.

I must go, and I will find.
That special place, that special me.
From the garden to the sea.
Where I can find, where I can be.

The Sky

I drove away
without looking back,
from now on
there will be no lack.

I will plant my garden
with beautiful seeds,
I will not be afraid
to remove all the weeds.

Yes! The little voice shouted.
My candlelight was getting brighter;
my fears and my
tears were getting lighter.

I turned on the radio
and started to sing.
Pink flowers, white flowers,
what joy they will bring.

Darkness was descending;
what a beautiful sky.
A clear, deep blue with
all the stars twinkling by.

I parked my car
on a lonely road,
I went outside
I need it to unload.

I climbed on the
hood of my car.
The sky so close,
yet the stars so far.

The hours went by,
watching the heavens above.
I was filled with the wonder
of true peace and love.

The feelings inside me
filling my future with hope.
Giving me strength,
telling me I could cope.

That I AM somebody
and I was meant to see,
all the beautiful things
that can make my life free.

I was meant to travel to
many different roads.
West, north, east, and south.
Handling different loads.

I was meant to see and be
many different things.
To learn from them
and let them fill up my being.

I knew I was
traveling the right way,
and vowed to listen to
what the little voice had to say.

I must go, and I will find.
That special place, that special me.
From the garden to the sea.
Where I can find, where I can be.

The Road

I wanted to get there
as fast as I could,
the sea will be waiting.
I knew that it would.

I drove away,
the time flying by.
Wait a minute!
Life is passing you by.

You did not pay attention
to all the beautiful sights,
you passed all those towns
and never saw the bright lights.

What is the matter with you?
Slow down your pace,
open the window, and
let the air caress your face.

Let the beauty surround you,
your spirit sublime.
Let yourself go;
take one step at a time.

Live in the moment,
and you will feel more alive.
Do not get impatient,
I AM sure you will survive.

Life is filled with journeys
from the start to the end.
It is the middle that counts;
it will count in the end.

Your garden will still be there
and so will the sea,
lookout for new seeds
and let yourself be.

Watch where you're going;
focus your eyes.
Stay on your truth
and forget all the lies.

I kept on going
at a much slower pace.
I wanted to be part of the
things staring at my face.

I wanted to listen,
I wanted to live truly.
In the end, I could say
I lived my life fully.

The road came to an end;
the hotel was in sight.
The sea close by,
I made it. "All right!"

I parked my car
and got my things out,
"I AM here. I AM here."
I wanted to shout.

I must go, and I will find.
That special place, that special me.
From the garden to the sea.
Where I can find, where I can be.

The Hotel

I walked towards the lobby
it was empty inside,
except for a lonely clerk
who looked like she wanted to hide.

I felt the same way,
I tried to make it quick.
But there were many rooms,
Which one should I pick?

I picked the one with an ocean
view; it was easier for me.
Closer to the path
where I could finally find me.

The clerk rang a bell
my heart skipped a beat.
Relax, it's ok. Go
ahead and take a seat.

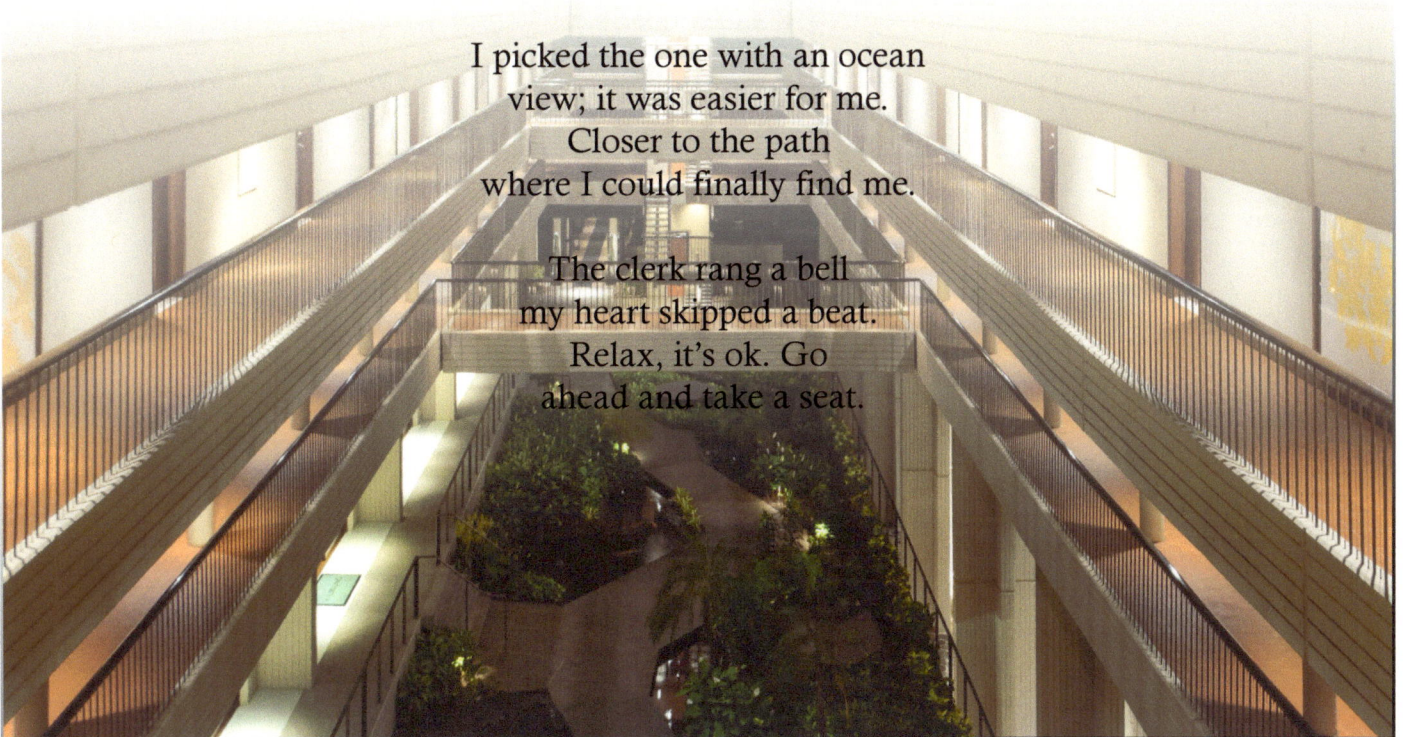

I knew I was nervous
my poor little hands,
waiting to touch
the white skin sands.

The bell boy showed up
and walked me to my room.
I walked inside;
there was no cloud of doom.

The curtains were open
the sea calling my name.
I knew from now on
nothing will be the same.

I said goodbye to the bellboy
and sat down on a chair.
I opened the window to let
my face feel the air.

I sat there staring
at the beautiful moon,
I will walk to the
ocean sometime soon.

The room felt cold,
but it was only temporary.
It was good to move on
and not always be weary.

Tonight was the night
to let go of the past,
to build a better future
where love really lasts.

My eyes filled with tears
there was a glimpse of sadness,
but as the light shone
I was filled with gladness.

I laid down on the bed
and closed my eyes tight.
Listening to the waves,
waiting for the light.

I must go, and I will find.
That special place, that special me.
From the garden to the sea.
Where I can find, where I can be.

A Dream

I opened my eyes
and looked around,
there was nothing there,
no walls, not even the ground.

I could feel myself
floating up to the sky.
I could see cities, oceans,
mountains passing me by.

I tried not to panic,
for this must be a dream.
I could see in the distance
a familiar gleam.

I didn't know what was happening,
yet I did not have a care.
It seemed very normal,
an everyday fare.

The gleam was getting closer,
I didn't have any fear.
Happiness filled my whole being
and not a tear.

I felt like I belonged there
in that faraway place.
I didn't have a name, for
it defied time and space.

I finally got there;
my heart opened wide.
Everything was beautiful from
top to bottom and side to side.

There were all kinds of flowers
in neat little rows.
White picket fences
with little pink bows.

Different lights. White,
violet, green, and blue.
Shining from my being,
Yes! It was all true.

Everything was beautiful
I could see it all shine;
this was my true place.
Mine, only mine.

True happiness filled me.
The Secret Place from above
that shined also within me
with true peace and love.

It was time to leave,
but I knew I would be back.
To this beautiful place
where I could keep track.

This was my garden,
filled with faith and light.
Filled with love and peace,
Yes, this was me. All right!

I must go, and I will find.
That special place, that special me.
From the garden to the sea.
Where I can find, where I can be.

The Sea

I opened my eyes,
my mind was clear.
I knew I had found
that place without fear.

It had been inside me
since the beginning.
I need it to wake up
to begin seeing.

I got out of bed
and started to get ready.
My heart was excited;
my thoughts were steady.

I walked outside
my senses flourished.
My heart and soul
were completely nourished.

My hands! Warm and tingling.
My rich little hands,
touching the soft
white skin sand.

A wave of happiness
filled my whole being.
This beautiful place
that I was truly seeing.

The air caressed my face;
it smelled really good.
No more wondering
where I once stood.

I forgave myself
for all the past misery.
I knew the future
was still a mystery.

I was in the right place
and time. It was all right;
the candle within me
was shining bright.

The new seeds for my
garden where being planted.
I will take my life and
lessons no more for granted.

"I AM very proud of you,"
said the loud voice.
"You remembered who you are, and
you will always have a choice."

I went swimming in the water,
"Yeah!" I shouted, really loud.
Living in the moment,
I felt humbled and proud.

I had completed one journey
of many more to come.
Waiting for another one,
soon it will come.

I have gone, and I have found.
That special place, that special me.
From the garden to the sea.
Where I have found where I AM me.

THE END...

Notes

www.ingramcontent.com/pod-product-compliance
Lightning Source LLC
Chambersburg PA
CBHW042247100526
44587CB00002B/51